ANTLER DAN'S RULE
poems new & selected

by

Donald Lee

Riverbank Books
2095 CR 3259
Clarksville, AR 72830
donthepoet@yahoo.com

(Some of these poems appeared previously in separate collections: NO AIR ON THE MOON, BEHIND THE ELF HEAD, and RARA AVIS.)

Cover illustration by Vincent Van Gone

Publication of this book was made possible thru a generous grant from the Scranton Arts Council, over across the Bridge: Darryl Johnson, Heather Lynn Waits, and Megan Nicole Miller.

To Absent Friends:

Jim Tesch
Rob Edwards
W. H. Pugmire
Joe Pulver
Ray Faraday Nelson
C Ra McGuirt
Phyllis Johnson
Melody Rust

"If it's a word, it's not an animal. And if it's an animal, its voice won't reflect light, so you can escape its language."

~ Barton Smock

TABLE OF CONTENTS

RIVERBANK POEMS

KARMA

For every hour you spend
Atop an Aztec pyramid
At Teotihuacan, far above
The arid landscape,
The Pyramid of the Moon
In the near distance,
You must spend exactly one month
In county lock-up back home,
Surrounded by fellow screw-ups
As far out of your own orbit
There as you were high up
Looking down at the stone jaguars
And tiny human ants ascending
The steps to your summit far below.

DINER POEM 5 A.M.

Morning rattles again
Takes a deep breath
Stirs up some early light
Along the street, blue
A little, as if a hand
Somewhere had thrown a switch
The sound rising to meet
The blue dawn light
Venus there suddenly remembered.

CAT WAR MANIFESTO

For it seems Mr Pickles
Loves blue cheese,

Loves it like a gun loves murder
Loves it like that Dobbs Ferry Rat,

That bastard his day will come
Hard and fast he keeps at

Our cheese our bowl
Laid out late of night

By Mr Big House Man
For us, not for that

Damned Dobbs Ferry Rat
Our crunchy feast

Nor Old Possum Jones
Who's Mr Guts and plays dead

When caught mouth full
Of our grub, our crunchy bowl

Ours not theirs, ours,
Our blue cheese:

Kill kill kill!
I see things from
The under side now.

HOW I MET YOUR MOM
(Marlboro Lite 100's in the Box)

I used to know this girl
Would let you suck her toes
For a pack of smokes--

Nineteen year old girls
Smell like Hope, for sure
She did and when she'd

Hit a pause in talk
She'd shout, "I'm telling Mom!"
Which knocked me down

On the floor laughing--
She went to Oregon
Last I heard. Wotta doll.

MANITOBA SONNET

My beautiful militant lesbian
Feminist pal from Manitoba
Was couch-surfing thru Arkansas
And stayed a few days with
An old gal at a commune over
Near Brashhears, said they
Were making dinner and her
Host was trying to open a jar
Of home-made pickles but
It refused to budge so she
Finally looked at it in disgust
And said, "Fucking men,"
And put it back on the shelf
And they had store-bought instead.

HOT AFTERNOON

If you take an empty
Forty-two oz bottle of Olde
English "800" malt liquor
Cap it and sit cross-legged
Up to your chest naked in
An oldschool swimming hole
Surrounded by placid murk (cold)
Jade green water dragonflies
And pissed-off squirrels up the
Hill the hot round rocks on the
Bank beyond your shade and
If you pull that empty bottle
All the way down and let it go
It will shoot up as high as
Three feet in the air, or
So I'm told.

BOOT CAMP POEM/FORT GORDON GEORGIA

Drill sergeant said
Stay off Broad Street
But they went on down
That Saturday past
Tattoo parlors
Massage parlors
Pizza parlors
To a bar with
Cheap beer, met
Up with these two
Fine gals who said
Let's ride out to
Our place in the country-
Side for fun, took the dudes
Way out of town
Robbed 'em both
Left 'em on the road-
Side in their BVDs
And turned out
They weren't really
Even girls at all.
Not that there's anything
Wrong with that.

MEXICO CITY POEM

I flew away disgraced that day,
December/cold

My ruined jeep crushed
In Dad's front yard which

He took with poor grace
Rolled in a ditch by

This young gal I was
Teaching how to drive my stick

So I hiked out on foot
At first daylight down

The Hwy 71 to the runway
Where my flight took off

At eight, and half an hour
Before the big jet hit the

Upper drafts, tear-eyed
And worried sick, my mom

Showed up with sandwiches
In a sack in her mother's way

And so I fled the snow and deep dismay

WHAT GOD IS?

Under the bridge saw Chuck Hazen
And his gal gave me a Busch Lite
Like always and she told me
About her troubled niece age 16
An *Atheist* now out of control!
What the actual hell to do?
I said make her a list:

God is a tree.
God is a perfect cloud.
God is a cute boy's ass
On a Saturday night at
The Quik-e-Mart

God is a kitten or
When you have a crap day
You call a pal who
Knows the right thing to say

God is NOT church
Not rules nor clothes
Not pass-the-plate when
You're broke as hell

Nor the approval of old folks
You don't know and never will:
But God is up yonder someplace
Someplace for Real

So keep your chin up Little Sister
You are well-loved Despite All.

I guarantee.

NEW ORLEANS UPPER NINTH WARD 2007

If I could fly back thru time
I might hang on a little longer
To that cute young hooker
With the leopard skin panties
Who sneaked back in my place
When my wife came down to
Talk me into moving home
And stole her purse and all
Her credit cards and $40
And all I could say was
Wow Honey crime sure is bad
Around these parts! Her name
Was Amber. She was a country girl.

ONE WIFE MAY HIDE ANOTHER
(after Kenneth Koch)

One girl may hide a different girl
As one costume may hide a
Different costume come Halloween
Or as one love may hide
A second love, which you
Do not see because you cannot
See behind love
Then one finds the second love
Hiding behind the other,
Served in secret, just as
One wife may hide another wife,
One who lingers there waiting,
Waiting for the wife to slip,
To give her then a helpful push,
To see how long she falls and falls
Before you hear her bounce.

TIME

The riverbank at Scranton,
The horizon's the line of trees
Across the channel and
Down the levy road past
Where it ends abruptly in sand
Horizon's shrink in time I guess
"A portfolio of diminishing expectations"
My uncle from out in Indio
Said he felt closed in back here
Trees hemming you in
Whichever way you turned
Not like the open desert
The rolling dunes
Palm trees and
The Salton Sea
Shrinking every
Day

SLEEP OVER

I love it when
You tug my beard
That look you give
Your elbow nudge

At four a.m.
I punch your pillow
Shift and turn
You snort and kick

Your breath is hot
Upon my throat
Your cat descends
Upon my face

I'm in his spot
He knows his place.

And mine.

MAGA poem

Lacking frontal lobes,
The shark must
Avoid-fear-smear-hate
Slander-dominate-distort-delete
Anything it does not know
Understand or can't contemplate.

Don't forget to vote next November.

BREAKFAST IN AMERICA

Me a flea in a rented circus,
If I was a bridge I'd be on fire
But fun and tired and sad
Get home from work, a beer,
Sex it up with girlfriend,
Plus fight.

I love all this domestic crap:
I take it all too much to heart
It slashes all my tires and
I crack up in the ditch at
The edge of town, in my brain

Then two weeks later
She looks at me and
Says, why are you
Acting so weird?

ZEBRA MUSSELS

Zebra Mussels are small & hatchet shaped Zebra Mussels will attach to anything: boats, other mussels, turtles, crayfish, your mom, etc. Zebra Mussels have been found in many romantic locales: Lake Dardanelle, the St. Francis River, Bull Shoals, & Plum Bayou in Arkansas. And your mom. Zebra Mussels can live for days in moist, dark livewells and bilge areas, abandoned grain silos, and under your bed. And your mom. Transporting Zebra Mussels across state lines is a crime, but only for immoral purposes, so check for ID. If you find a Zebra Mussel, do not loan it money or introduce it to your mom. Northern Snakeheads are actually okay if you like to party.

POTUS 29

Warren G. Harding
Was at heart basically
A sweet, good-
Natured guy who
Couldn't say no
To his friends
And just wanted
To be loved.

Warren, his
Father had said,
If you were
A woman you'd
Be in a family
Way all the
God-damned time.

CAVEAT EMPTOR

"The one real bookstore in town is run by hideous fabulous monsters, sisters. A basilisk and a manticore. One keeps her eyeballs in a jar in her pocket and eats bugs; the other has a long wooden tail and lives on Hobo Fear Sweat and spinal fluid. Their feet leave singe marks where they walk. When they sneeze, little alien babies cry in their sleep on other planets. One out of 217 customers inevitably joins the statue garden located out back, frozen tears running down frozen cheeks. Plus no discount for locals. Zero stars out of five because the stars wink out in their baleful presence. No joke. Amazon delivers."

SNOWFLAKE

she talked out the side
of her mouth like a gangster
i think she did a lot of
coke back in the day --
she said, rub the lining
of yr nose raw with sandpaper
then take everything you own
out in the yard in a pile
and set it on fire:
that's cocaine

FOR MY FATHER (AFTER PHILIP WHALEN)

Being a modest man, you wanted
Expected an ordinary child
And here's this large, inscrutable object
ME
You recognize part of the works
Ones you first donated in 1962
But what are they doing?
The transmission slips, and

Was there a warranty? Doubtless not.
Why couldn't it be more like a
Farm truck, or a sports car? Something.
Not this baroque moneypit
Which with great elaboration, gears
Spinning and too much flash of the wrong sort,
Produces a thing like this, words,
Sometimes worth $ to folks in New York, or not,
Nobody knows why.

POEM FOR THE LOVELY LESBIAN FROM MANITOBA I SAW AGAIN THIS WEEK

my roommate said
"not only is she
not thinking of you
tonight, she is
in fact imagining
a utopian realm
somewhere far away
and wonderful yet
totally devoid of Penis."

well, hell.

XILITLA

a green mountain like
a young girl's breast
hangs over tin roof'd xilitla

thru the mist green parrots
the unpaved road with chickens
the singing girls inside the school

descent to the bottom
where the children played ball
and stared at me gape-mouthed

washed shirts would not dry
on the line overnight
in the sierra gorda

the tethered goat sways
on the roadside in the grass
La Silleta, the mountain, looms above

SONNET FOR MY GRANDMOTHER

Death, where are thy 10,000 stings?
My father knows, leaning down to speak.
My son (11), standing by her bed
At one end of the span
Smiles widely for my grandmother
Who's at the other, her thoughts
Always on her face.
Dark water rushes underneath.

She herself waiting for that doorway
Into that perfect cloudless moonlit night
Where my grandfather waits,
Wrinkles sweetly smoothed by hand,
Feeds the hens & chickens,
Wonders what's keeping her so long.

crickets outside and rain. slept 11 hours. diet dr.
pepper. brain hurts. today my life consists of: a
ceiling fan with a broken blade, the sound of rain, no
money. books. unrequited love. a taxi shift every
day at 5. drunken sorority girls who overtip. a tarot
card (the prince of wands: "intensity; blossoming
love; intuitive creativity; out of darkness into light"--
maybe). absent friends. poems. the girl with the
limp who never tips and always tells me what movie
she just saw. she doesn't like pretty actresses. they
"annoy" her. i try to imagine what her life is like.
staying on top of the movies like that must be a full
time job.

SONNET AFTER JOHN WIENERS

The poem does not lie to us. We
Live under its law. The morning sun
On the window reflects it on the
Motes of dust in the air. The smell
Of the coffee and the sound of the
Passing car. Somewhere a dog barks.
It is too easy to sit here and wonder
Why I do this. The dog's bark is
More meaningful than mine is.

The coffee gives us hope. The dog
Barks because it must, that is
Its job. It punches a clock also.
The motes of dust make their
Own days as they coalesce together.
I hide a poem under my tongue.

MERCURY DIMES

O God, O Venus, O Mercury,
Patron of thieves, give me in
Due time, I beseech you,
A million bucks. A cruise to
Old Atlantis. A sunny wife
With wings and perfect pitch.
A car with fins. Good boots.
Homer Simpson's actual battered
Copy of the I-Ching, notes and all.
A tattoo of the 1968 cover of
"Indian War Whoop" by the
Holy Modal Rounders. Good teeth.
A double date with Betty AND Veronica.
Sea monkeys that endure. World Peace.
O God, O Venus, O Mercury,
Be the loose change you want
To see in this wicked weary world:
Brother can you spare a dime?

SOME GIRLS

HURRICANE JAMIE

I think of you like
Grace Kelly or sea storms--
Gone, Cape Hattaras!
Gone, St. Augustine!
Gone Atlanta, Gone Raleigh!
Gone, Bayonne & Fire Island!
All swept away by
Your eyes & mouth
Then flying madly
Into your arms --
But often, in the Eye
It is calm

POEM

coral or old wine
i can't look out the
window without
hearing you run
up the stairs in a
rush to give me
that welcome
shuffle knock
o my girl of the
evening primroses!

HEADLONG INTO THE FLAME

it brings terrible risks (they warn)
i do not see them, only currents
of fire and air consuming me
gladly here now

it is ordinary, like smoke
although i cannot sleep
and long to burn the cities
of the earth in your name

or lay roses at your feet
love and drink and song
a madrigal to you o mine
fair damoiselle, dark like the burning sun

HOW ENTIRELY MORTAL IS THE LOVE I BEAR FOR YOU

forgive me, i am dazzled
by your sorrow darling
girl! washed away by all
this icy rain, caught up in it

my world's the blue crown
on the throne of my
kingdom of yearning, there
forg'd by tongs of hunger for you

holy and fine the pulse of
breath on your lips each
day, hope roaring out from
my excellent prayers toward you

and yet it's you. you. i ache
for love of the holy and luminous
sea, which is you, which is
the dawn there above the waves

XMAS POEM

For my sins I live in the city of Fayetteville--
Everything is clear from here at the center
To the end of my block, I can see thru the trees
Past the house with the mannequins
At seventy miles an hour--
This is my certain place, a pleasant smell of
Apples often fills the air.

June night exists, June night exists,
Even here in our December and the rain--
O you who are wrapt in velvet
Drop by sometime with a peach
In one hand & a firefly in the other,
Come sing old Cole Porter songs to me--

OARS TUCKED

You go too far, but what to do?
The trees are indifferent to each of us,
The faces of virgins white boats, oars tucked

Waiting (Your being beautiful, say,
Younger than the trees, morning
Fed on explicit song: the other

Morning a clue to the question of
My angel which I take enormously
Seriously. You should know. To know this

You can navigate the river of night.
Think about it. Strange birds sing
Red-faced and shy, a regular fleet in

Expectation. I love this strange life.
I love crying in the kitchen, what am I
To do now? Call me please when you get this.

ALBA LONGA

Women get under things. In the shadow
Of the pink moon carving ice like the
Night sky, ice grinding stone,
Carving strange signs there into it.

Never the same later. Wouldn't want to be.
Flesh is real, transitory, we are made
Of it. The marks show. Even in the
Dim moon light, even then, if you look.

Looking back, almost seen, never quite.
Finger tips feel the grooves in it--
Trace ahead, try to guess. Never guess.
It never shows that way. Flesh is frail.

POEM NOT BEGINNING WITH A LINE FROM PINDAR

By their high & ancient light
You saw the nature of yourself--
You are not a pinnacle
Of creation beneath a protected
Veil of sky, you are
A fierce bright atom of
Self-hood encircled by fire.

I stand in doubt, surrounded
By holy wood--it is this
Hand hiding in smoke,
A cherry button heart,
A blazing circle of rum--
You are here, shaping
Suns & arrows, a halo
Of moon-rays, bright at 2 a.m.

Thing is to cut a shape in time,
A shape that's the shape of you--
No goddess, you must be revived,
Devin among the grasses--
Hearts revive with you:
Every moment then is light.

BIRTHDAY 38 POEM

Puerto-Rican girls are terrific!
But I don't know any
Puerto-Rican girls
Here in the pool hall:

I will pretend you are
The Puerto-Rican girl--
You look that good
In your little dress
And your eyes sparkle chica!

SONNET AFTER ALICE NOTLEY

Certain gestures repeat endlessly in recollection.
It is night and you are sleeping. The big cold
Night is singing softly to itself. In my dream
You are on a balcony--there is sea-air
And bougainvillea. Now in the alley I am
Singing to myself--I hear the night sing too.
I am alone in the wet and purple night, so sweet
Like air, and not discontent: hands in pockets, happily
cold.

We got our feet wet in things, didn't we? and so are
Formed like angels, like bougainvillea. Really
I'm glad. Certain gestures repeat endlessly
In recollection, in dreams. My shoes scuff
The paving stones, marked by moonlight. You are marked
By moonlight, too--so sweet like air, so fair.

SONNET

At a party I went because,
I went because I don't go enough,
Out, usually I just go home, I do
Remember distinctly faces, music--
Across the house you were there
I saw you elegant in furs distinctly
There poised I thought in the distance
Across the faces past them on the other side.
I thought standing across the house
By the music then mostly of your
Lavender sock, and mostly then
I wished I had it back, and was
Back home looking right then at it
On my chair.

NEW POEM FOR SABRINA

Medea's a Phoenician wench, Sabrina's
Pasadenan/ hails from boulevards &
Constellations, surface undersea Galaxies
Near the beach

My world has made/ an Oriental turn
Meaning: mysterious! orphic! fun!
And I walk my day on Fu Manchu
Standard Time/ Have come to
A fork in the road/ & am taking it

Things whip toward the center
Sweeping me down/ to the floor
After my Odyssey up & later
Further down below

My angels were losing/ patience,
Christmastime so near, trees
Standing stark naked/ On my street
In a line. It is December 6. I'm 39.

GREEN RING

sweet perfection of you
in all its vagaries
alongside mine, alongside
me in bed, in the store,
in the kitchen, you are
a myth within my heart

LAST NIGHT THOUGHTS (for R.L.S.)

Caterpillar, mirror or tomb--
You're a brand-new sky
To hang the stars upon tonight

Idiosyncratic & particular,
Like language itself--
Your ashtray is full like my heart

Guys my age
Ride bikes for health--
I drink 40s in my car

Aetherial spirit bright as morning
Water blue as November dawn--
I are not a 42 year old (un)/happy poet

The deer on the hill
Console me. I'm behind
In my life

What is patriotism but
All the good things
We ate in childhood?

Music on the car radio,
A river in the distance
Marked by a line of trees

Pink stucco, traffic, broken
Loveseat. Weight bench, notebook,
Robin. Plants in sun. Robin. Robin.

PERSONAL POEM

Every possible thought charged with sudden
Meaning, loose high energy, leaves skittering
In a gust American Beauty-style across the pavement
Like little children, laughing, then up up a big
Yellow lemon balloon into the blue wide sky
Right out of sight. Terrific!
Out of two eyes gazing amazed and welcoming at
Me, up late, impossible to misplace
Under this light and anticipated light--
Not: come live on the floor with me, she said, and I
Did--she didn't say that, but I would, I would.

BREAKFAST SONNET

The temple of your volcanic kiss is burning,
Edges charred, smoky air, submission
To an unfinished heart. Such comeliness
Flares cobalt blue, lemon, carmine red
Against my dull tones, fog and sand.
What night fenced in is poised between us,
Towering above the rest, above your
Curtained air, above my giltless charm,

River-daughter, real as you are real,
Hitting upon things--the chair, the cup--
Behind our studied loveliness, a flame-
Hurling devil angel, not unwelcome here--
Buried certain fathoms beneath the earth,
And above, down the abandoned heaven to us now.

NO AIR ON THE MOON

Late at night he hustles wine,
Believes in things--"Baffling combustions
Are everywhere!" In my backpack,
In Heidi's sweater, across town off Garland Ave.
In my x-girlfriend's ill-used spice rack!
In this Friday slush I stride through
Off-balance and stern.

Four walls mean something (others have noted this),
We make love to pretty girls when we have time,
Otherwise stomp Lyrically across the wet & purple day
When on fire, like now, pregnant w/ mandrakes
& making "vast apple strides" toward the ice floes.
Caught up in the talons of a gigantic eagle, a really
big One, the biggest one of all!

"It is winter. We are here. AND THERE IS NO MONEY."
My dream a nest of light & heat, the 2 a.m. quilts &
Rain at the windowpane & Love: "real as keyholes,
Real as affadavits"--

The trouble with comparing a Poet to a '64 Mercury
Comet:
Comets don't develop scar tissue blazing across the sky
At 2 a.m. like a remonstrance--

But you will.

MERMAID THIRSTY

In the tidepool of memory / flooded, the salmon
hover, gills moving in the still clear water,
subsisting on scraps in a distant room--
Regret is a series of sadly foregone /
Conclusions / a cold isle in a northern sea--

[Now] here I am at my
Desk / driving along the winding shore road
in search of : Melody Ritter, Katie McCauley,
Wilma Shively, Patty Warfel, / Carol Rhatigan.
Even Maefern Shroeder! Dolores Sneathern! Helen
Tidmarsh!
[loudly:] Where are you girls? I am alone in the wet &
purple light. / Plodding through the sand / Loose
sand & these lousy goddamn shoes--

Whose wet swimsuit there by the tree
And small damp footprints going
Out to sea

LOVE-POEM AGE 37, 26:III:2000

a desire now to go out into the light,
wobbly, blinking, trying to remember,
unshaven, to take with grace long breaths
of chilled blue morning air, like wine--

replete, somehow, sinew'd, girt for the
labours ahead: a desire to be of use, in
short, to the actual exercise of innocence
in a complex situation little aided
by theory.

THE CATS IN ANNIE'S ALLEY

the cats in annie's alley / annie who
broke the blue jeep with freckled hands /

down her alley / in florida i guess
where one sometimes goes "i wish i

were there" / or had gotten just one
pearly kiss / for the jeep

SHE STAPLED THE WING BACK ON THE ANGEL

I swing the words, electric around the Gotta life
toward the syntax of your smooth thighs & Summer knees
dancing, flooding the room with light

candle apple breasts & the slightest
hint of blue lace panties; this salty decade
my ruins, broken stone, like a postcard found in an old
book

paperclip pretensions: real as you are not real, enticing--
(the biological bureaucracy files its damned charts)
formless summers, a book of wet matches, flat beer

outcast on a cold & distant shore

GARDEN FULL OF CHARM

They are very shallow people who take every
thing literally / but not us, *we* don't!--
Fiddle tunes in our sandy hearts! / Whiskey,
my girl! my men need whiskey!

Let the music from the kitchens ruin my heart
Let onion atoms lurk within the bowl
If I come away with salt in my beard
As dark as the hours we have tasted,
I remain: alive in my old black boots, car keys,
Harry Smith records, keenly anticipating

The curve of your thigh on my couch /
Pale in the pale moonlight

POEM FOR 3 WOMEN

deadheading roses, withered petals cut away--
dark eyes, perfect criticisms, big ecstasy
settled, bill paid, put away, almost forgotten--
surprise! but no autobiography ignores crucifictions

were you trying to paint over shadows?
the wine & mediterranean arches
like a coal kept banked for morning,
pale in the pale moonlight

my delightful emperor is like cool rain,
a crazy uncle wanting to get laid--
(I touched her bra-strap when I hugged her goodbye,
my hand tingled for 1/2 an hour)

these longings surprise me: promiscuous fireflies!
a river, one arbitrary red barnacle on the hull of old
memory

LENTEN POEM

Fat Tuesday Lent has begun
Here by the bottom of the rainbow, like
A cast-off shirt Across town
She is in bed with aflame and
Fun 2:27 a.m. She mentioned
mentioned despondent this guy She
Called like I really wanted to hear about
Called despondent this guy At
The bottom of the rainbow Tonight the
Stars are like a crowd of faces of faces
Faces lips pressed tight Across
Town Lent has begun Like a
Cast-off shirt like an old suitcase she
Can just drag around Her legs
They ought to be on stamps Across town
She is in bed with a coffinful of angel
Wings me I don't fly too good
Anymore The butterfly on the
Wheel across town across she is in
Bed 3:00 a.m. the best time to listen
To NPR cool sibilant voice like sangria
An old suitcase she can just drag
Around Be my icon she said
Tuesday the canal waters of Fayetteville
I cling to my paddle watching the
Mermaids swim past endlessly
Across town my candy heart snaps
Across town she is in bed She is in bed with
Go she said:
Go down and peer among the fishes
she said Lent
has begun.

571-4309

Look, my dear friend, look:
Situations arise, despite
Our least intentions, of
Which I was one,
I guess, doubtless.
Still: I love you, a constant--
Please someway understand
The passing nature of such
Eternal Call Song &c.
So: again, I' m
home, so
call

BALL LIGHTNING

The telephone keeps ringing & ringing--
Love comes in a sort of sly & winking way
& goes, the wooden clack of pigeon wings
across the grass & past the bluegreen hedge.

Ha-Ha it's so fun to run out on the long front porch
The winter moon (the cat's-claw moon) & she,
slamming her car door & bounding up the stairs--

Thank god we're living in the future now,
everything has a kind of metallic sheen
to it, did you not notice? That's how you know
it's future now, she never understood that part.

Boss Poet, stumped by her cold balk--
I may be the fool she limns each night
(our pillow talk) yet if it's so I remain
Happily poised.

She squeezed the universe into a ball
& then pronounced its lack. It isn't her world,
She's living in her own future now--& besides,
She said, I don't read Poems anymore.

The telephone keeps ringing & ringing-
I can't believe you're 37 she said again
(Well Christ, I thought, if it were just
a matter of that)

BIRTHDAY POEM FOR SABRINA

I wanna roo you from two til four,
Until your seminar. I know it's hardly
Fair: Me Tarzan, Heap Big Intellectual--
You Jane, Full of Mysteries--I know you
Put on socks & hate Wal-Mart (& shop
there anyway) like everyone else. But you are
Bubblicious, Buddy! I light a clove & watch you
On the stair, your legs they ought to be on stamps!
My bounty in other words is boundless as the sky,
In the land where they have the Big Sky; or the front
Lawn of St. Elizabeth's Catholic Church, the one
You enter thru the steeple, up below the Crescent Hotel--
Shady & full of squirrels.

So: I'll water the fern, I'll read your kid to bed--
Dig thru the books for something I've not read,
Doze on the couch til you get back.
(Your valentine candy heart said, "Be my icon,"
It was *mine* that said, "In the middle of the
River of our lives, the long sounds of trains
Reach to us across the silent moving waters."
I like yours best.) And now your footstep
On the stair comes like a piece of dream, & in
Their windowbox, the bougainvillea
Shift their roots in keen antici-
pation.

TIBETAN LOVE SONNET

I'm still on the mountain,
Kept away from you by
Avalanche, snow leopard,
All manner of time & space--

I love the very idea of you
So right, the cricket in the corner
Of my tent beside the lantern
Sings your song.--

The sherpas speak of you
In whispers in their tongue
Of Shangri-La which I do not
Understand,--

The midnight moon which shines
On me this evening shines on you.

LOVE,

your
face
the center
in a series
of rushing
water over rocks
in the stream-bed
of my real morning
awake 1/2 dressed
sensibility
where
you now
lie glinting
in the cataract clear
and pure as I mug at
my reflection and love you

POEM

To wake up with
A girl in my bed
Flickering like a
Green candle flame
In the sheets
Bare foot exposed
Pink tipt naked

Kiss me down
Into your memory
Beauty I wasn't
Born high enough
For you

AS I DRIFT DOWN

today wild green parakeets
on the tree-shadow'd deck
screaming
love in the trees
on tv
I make the gesture
here, and elsewhere
carved in runes indecipherable
all trace out your name

THINKING OF "THE BLUE ROSE SONNETS"

thinking of "the blue rose sonnets,"
up late, I know how Columbus felt,
a secret route to the Indies, etc.,
the Holy Grail, which is you, the
Plus-Ultra!, & just because it
turns out to be Florida don't mean jack!
I mean, Okefenokee is okay, too,
and if *you* turn out to be real, too,
get pissed off at times, throw your
stuff all over the place, I can
revel too in flying plates and tearful reconciliations.

POEM FOR HEIDI AND HER BABY

zammis watches me
as I leave
he's seeing things
that no one else can see

everything is a-ok:
his mama's very beautiful today

DEVIL GIRL

because of those crazy heels
she was wearing

with her little lace
red devil dress

I carried her all around
outside that night

at the party
with her in my arms

for well over an hour
and her eyes sparkled

when I set her down at last
near the laundry room

EX-WIFE POEM

she disapproves
of the way leaves fall
from the trees
when they fall in my yard

A CATALOGUE OF YOUR CHARMS

You are the brightest apple of my afternoon--
green, blue, some kind of, like, *burgandy* birdsong.
You are more important than sleep.

You are a small song in the wilderness
You are a dovetail joint,
You are the honeybee mouth I coil'd my tongue around.

Ass of Venus! (the first champagne goblet
was molded from the breast of Helen of Troy;
the second one was you)

*"Sorry I can't be more help in--not solving the
mystery of woman--but what? helping you
find a woman who allows you to look at her clues"
--letter from Cone Turner*

"You are a Major-General in the marching band
of the Heroes of the Republic".

Someday you will be on a coin.

You are the chocolate-covered raisin of my morning,
the hottest band this side of the iron curtain,
a blue train ride, a stroll in the rain, the silence
of ten thousand crickets:

A halo of moon-rays, rolling downhill,
bright as day at 4 a.m.

I'D LOVE TO BE YOU

September rolls like a wave over
Our cuffs, strains of Tchaikovsky
Hanging in the air. The word is not
The thing. Countries get crazy &
Go to war all week long.

Despair of hangdog love, her sunny
Lust buoys me up & then I go
Crashing down. Boom. Legs broken,
Collarbone, dying in a hail of
Gunfire in front of the Biograph.

Form dictates content. I'd love
A day in bed with her form.
Maybe next week. Roper of stars,
To be joyous is to be a madman
In a world of sad ghosts. Ha!

OCTOBER POEM

Red Bud Inn, Mountain View, Ark.
Rain tonight, out,
Silent sidewalk town
Who knows solitude
Of the polar night
In this dank burg?
The girl at Hardee's sweeping
Glad to see my ass go out the door.

I don't want to take a walk
Or read someone else's book,
I want to make love to you
In a field of wild flowers,
But you aren't here.

Something in the delirium
Of the night hours,
I am a universe etc.
I'm happy with our hermetic games--
(Do you love me
Despite prevailing conditions?)

Rough, beautiful intoxication of you,
Poetickal,--Breakfasting on rain,
I think of your eyes.

ANN POEM

Ann is sad today,
Or seems so,
Cheek pillowed in hand
And hair all willow'd
Down, sipping her straw
Cigarette idly smoking
In her palm and
That's all I know.

LIGHT CLASSICS

BELLY MUSIC

I have written lines on the edges of your pages sweet
friend giving it a quality both humorous & romantic.
(The combination of harpsichord with seagulls I never
would have thought of in a million years, but it works
on you.)

I can't get out of this green city of clocks. Sorry.
You are here for one thing, I'll show you when you
come over. Everybody is young & they have beautiful
babies you can see at the edges of photos.

We should hang out more. At least Christmas is sexy
here, all wooden & gauzy & full of Americans (*grin*).

But I digress. I am beside you thru the ghost of
winter, hungry lions, you are a landscape I navigate
daily. Trees & the sound of a river running. Some
river! Amor fati. Optimism is a revolutionary act.

WHO ARE YOU? THE KEEPER OF SILVER GALOSHES?

Silence sharpened pencils
In the street & afterward
We managed to speak
Of coriander & dialogue
And the void, a dead man
Shaking out linen--yes
Unmade beds, the stars,
Your mouth, yes--
It quit raining & we just
Sat around.

POEM WRITTEN WHILE READING CLARK COOLIDGE

"You write from what you don't know
Toward whatever can be picked up in
The act
I think I was thinking
Eureka Springs is lovely though
Small & cheap

I am letting my beard go & go
It is a certificate of something
Around here like liking Chelsea's
Or the Lumberyard it's one or
The other me I hate the Lumberyard
Don't you?

The trees on my hill
Frame my weltanschaaung
As I go along
And come back to them
(And Frank Black, the leaf
Rain, the cell phone--)
Never alone.

DREAM-POEM

I dreamt I was taken
Within sight of a lighthouse
On a beach--in the dream
I remembered a trip to Florida
I took, that I never took.
What can this mean?

Tomorrow is easy, really really easy,
But tonight I am curious about the light-
House, what does it signify there
Just within sight? They are having
An awfully great time there on the other side,
I can hear the sound of the music
Beyond the big dunes.

OOMPA LOOMPA

The overpowering day hits
Like a circus midget! like a
Monkey in a cowboy suit!
Like a chocolate-covered raisin!

All its entanglements like
The threat of a hummingbird:
Lemonheads! Junior Mints!
Red licorice handcuffs!

I gnaw my way to freedom--
Willie Wonka, watch yr
Back, Jack!

EUREKA SPRINGS IN SNOW

this is where I live
I knew it would be like this
still, with the trees moving
seven a.m.
crystal
water trickle on
windowpane
air hurts
small town
shut down
glaciation

LIGHTNING SANDWICHES

Life is more fragile than
It was in 1237
Who knows how many
Kids you had that died?
That may be our saving grace
To prolong our species
Because our species
Is definitely self-destructive.
Our brains are our problem.

Chief Seattle said,
"Don't talk trash till you've
Danced in my trailer,
How can you buy my land
Till you come to my trailer
To see my tattoos?"

(And she began to dance to
Big Smith in a circle in tight
Red corduroys with a glass
Of black & tan in her little hand)

Turkey
Day
Pot Luck
1:30

The Tibetan monks were in
Key West doing their beautiful
Sand mandalas & some punk
Came in & began kicking up
Their hours of exquisite, delicate

Work. The crowd went nuts,
Surged forward to rip this skinhead
Limb from limb. But the monks
Formed a human shield around him.
He had captured the essence of
Their philosophy of art (& life)
With his big leather boots.

BLUE PANTIES (after Wallace Stevens)

There is no deductible for these,
With their hips they push asunder
The blue panties.

In Texas the twisted possibilities
Unravel like the lace on
Blue panties.

Near this small town in Oklahoma
Far away from the whirlwind
Of big city life I think of
Her blue panties.

I could hear the confusion
In the background. She was unable
To find her favorite pair
Of blue panties.

All the pressure had been taken
Off him, thank god. He had remembered
What had become
Of the blue panties.

Some of the wildest poker parties
In the history of the region
Came about directly as a result
Of such blue panties.

A man and a woman
Are one.
A man and a woman
Wearing blue panties

Are one.

The Civil Air Patrol painted on the
Sides of their aircraft a single
Pair of shimmering blue panties.

The persistence of 135 years
Of engineering excellence
Led to the design of
Perfect blue panties.

My legs stretch out to the horizon,
Like Gertrude Stein coming to Radcliffe,
Or a mule's brain, cloudy and dangerous;
The velvety intersection's bloom,
Wispy like her wonderful blue panties.

DEDICATION

His little bird died
Which he'd fed every
Two hours all night long--
Earnestly, 12 yrs old,
He let it sleep upon his breast.
But it died.

We cried together
On the steps outside.
We buried it on the hillside
Solemnly,

Patted the soil very slowly
Around, and in his small hand
A scattering of seeds of flowers,
To mark the spot.

Poor bird, he said. Poor bird,
I said, and held his hand,
And sighed.

BOTTLE ROCKET WARS (sonnet)

Almost white granite with little stars
Still seeking the thrill
Delicious bliss in the ritual--
(Say something in God-language!)

"Joyful ants rest in the roof of my tree
Daughters of 1/2 seen worlds
A star creasing the sky, a lie
(While in our willful way,
We, in secret play)
O green birds!

Meanwhile green rain falls across Chinatown,
The smell of ozone on wet pavement.
Some people can't smell it when it rains:
It's worth all the rest to be able to.

OCEANOGRAPHIE OF THE HUMAN HEART

...that there is no mention of directions, a certain way of standing, to see just so, but not how to get there, nor what to do later, after it's over and has worked, or not worked, when you feel that tremendous sense of elation or crushing anti-climax, and wonder why you bothered at all--you will always find things that you were not looking for, birds or ghosts of them singing in your heart, poised, awaiting the call that never came. you cannot call them. but it's okay you wanted to.

BLUE THIRST

patterns of time
a cold glass of milk and
the moon's bright
falling towers tumbling

ice rattling late against the
window panes and, and
a passing car shushes
things made out of human talk

the quiet shatter of light
patterns of time flowing
colder than ice
in the night kitchen

"from RED WEATHER (in-progress)"

Drums in the pre-dawn. In my head my brain churns like
bald tires on a gravel road. Wantonly. There was so much I
wanted to say, *telephone* or *zebra* or *goddamn*. But I let it
go, like the Pope. *Ego te absolvo*. Antarctica all the way, &
that's if she's *lucky*.

All I had were the trees, which is a lot, & the birds,
especially that goddamned nutty-sounding kind, that jungle
bird. God. I wonder how all the other birds deal, like
someone who gets drunk at a party & won't shut up &
keeps on saying the most excruciating things. Hello, Mr.
Inappropriate Disclosure! Goodbye!

"...in the years they lived there, carrying on with books,
babies and endless conversation." If you make the space in
your life will events rush to fill it? Yet the war goes on. Is
this what it was like during The Crusades? You want to be
home with your hippie chick girlfriend, the baby crawling
on the kitchen floor, instead you're 2 knights down from
Richard the Lion-Hearted, poised to rain Christian terror
down upon the Turk.

Fuck this noise. Rusty armor, stale sweat, bad food. The
dog on the front porch, the whistling teapot, the hummus
& tabouli are far, far away. Coltrane on the stereo, flowers
on the windowsill.

The horse snaps its tail at a fly, jangles its harness. Dust &
heat.

RARA AVIS

Dear C.,

The lifestyle of the urban middle-class dropout art-gypsy makes us both shine like Archie McPhee glow-in-the-dark rubber cephalopods plus the tilted architecture around here turns everything pure as gale and mist washing my skull. I like your cat. Have your people call my people. I offer you, here, now, with love, the Ten Warning Signs of Bohemianism:

1. Odd Dress
2. Long Hair
3. Living For The Moment
4. Sexual Freedom
5. Have No Stable Residence
6. Radical Political Enthusiasms
7. Drink
8. Drugs
9. Irregular Work Patterns
10. Addiction To Nightlife

You are the wonderful. Waves and Blankets of Stars regard your every move. I am entering the earth as a street closes but it's your street and then, as you follow the map with an extended fingernail, tracing its route, our homes in transfigured space, the furniture (surely) like darts scoring triple twenties across the landscapes of our autobiographies. We cohabitate chapters XVII-XXIII. The interesting ones. See footnote 2(a). www.amazon.com gives your review four and a half stars. You are responsible for at least four. Thanks.
With us no other work but the genius of present life.

Best,
D.

I REMEMBER (after Joe Brainard)

I remember my dog Blackie.

I remember jumping off the piano when I was 4 trying to fly & hurt my nose. I thought the cape was what did it.

I remember wanting to be a cowboy when I grew up.

I remember my first girlfriend Kimberly JoAnn Farris, when I was in second grade. She was also my cousin Jeff's girlfriend. She used to hold hands with both of us at the same time.

I remember when cokes were fifteen cents.

I remember three channels on TV.

I remember trips to Indio, California, when I was a kid & how hot the sidewalk was if you went barefoot.

I remember visiting my cousins in Lawrence, Kansas, & a kid on the street out front offered me a Tic-Tac & I thought it was drugs.

I remember the first night I slept in the dorm in college when I was 17. I was scared.

I remember the first time I shaved. I felt very solemn. And chafed.

I remember proposing to my ex-wife. I had to do it twice in a row before she said yes.

I remember walking around Tulsa on my honeymoon holding hands.

I remember doing push-ups in the Army in the rain in the mud.

I remember falling in love with Katie McCauley so hard it gave me a nosebleed.

I remember the first time I saw a girl's breasts for real. I thought they would be like foam rubber or Stretch Armstrong or something.

I remember getting drunk with Tommy Jacques & going to see Katie McCauley at the girls' dorm. She wore a polka dot dress. We sang "Rosalita" to her. Tommy fell down on the lawn.

I remember working as a security guard when I was first married & making contraband sandwiches in the big institutional kitchen at 4 a.m.

I remember when I thought Royal Crown Cola was exotic.

I remember seeing "Raiders of the Lost Ark" thirty-seven times.

I remember my roommate Kevin when he was ten and I went to school with his dad.

I remember Heidi Widder when she was sixteen with braces. She was very beautiful & shy. I sneaked her wine at a party.

I remember when I turned 33 thinking I had outlived Jesus, Alexander the Great, and John Bonham of Led Zeppelin.

I remember when my parents put me to bed when I was a kid & how if I needed to get back up for a glass of water or something, how I was always secretly afraid that if I peeked into the 1967 living room where they were watching TV or playing cards with their friends, they would all have giant ant-heads or something.

WHAT W.W. DENSLOW DID WITH THE MONEY HE MADE ILLUSTRATING THE ORIGINAL *WONDERFUL WIZARD OF OZ* (1900)

He bought an island off the coast
Of Bermuda and crowned himself
King Denslow the First, with his native
Boatman as the admiral of his fleet
And his Japanese cook as prime minister.

He died on May 27, 1915, of pneumonia.

REFLECTIONS ON *THE SHAGGY MAN OF OZ* (1949)

I need the Shaggy Man's
Love magnet, man, magnet,
Mack--ack! Love magnet,
& I could drive up up up
Her street, & all her love would
Floooooooow down my way, down to
My street, flow on down to my neighbor-
Hood

(howls at yellow moon, all full tonight) / exit
stage right

DRINK ME

"Curiouser and curiouser!" cried Alice
(She was so much surprised, that
For the moment she quite forgot how
To speak good English). "Now I'm
Opening out like the largest telescope
That ever was! Good-bye, feet!"

(from "Red Weather, pt. II") (in-progress)

But not so, & here I now am
Outside at night, surrounded by
Chaucerian groves of greenblack trees
Chorus of night music, Brahms & frogs

If nothing happens it is possible
To make things happen; a binding
Together of the real between us,
Commanding large fields but cultivating small ones.

What stranger are you living for?
It is only amateurs who feel keenly
The loss of the sky, that gloss upon
The surface of sin.

Full moon out tonight,
Dance on the patio in its light--
Forty-one years old,
Feeling all right.

ON THE IMPORTANCE OF QUIXOTIC GESTURES

(after starting Tender Buttons)

wet sand in my skull, I wonder
how all the gestures here, and
the light of Bohemianism,
in window you cast about
in the genius of energy:
a mouth to fill it?

go, like a fly
jangles its route,
our being as we live thru them
the kinds of the window
of time, yes a cold glass
of energy, a street closes but me.

me, up with a girl in the
cycles thru knowing the cold,
open sea (it is yet the
tombs of human talk,
the quiet shatter of
things more important than cynicism)

not to lie to rain Christian terror
down from the kitchen floor
a state with a clock also
what do if I do it
would be here turns everything pure,
as I let it makes us hope.

POETRY BURNED ON TABLES

Now I walk through light of mother-of-
Pearl & God emerges in a minor
Key to coax me out, now, my
Ordinary life. No wife. I always
Thought it would be more some
Other way, less like this. Dumb clarity.

Everything magnificent & tough,
Pale December sidewalk light. I rise
Each day from the tomb of sleep,
Captain of my fate, knowing we don't
See that much. Some things are really
There. I try to do it right.

INLAND WESTERN

But that was years ago. is my concern
My lifetime listens to yours, written
On the plane. we are alive in an hour
Cold, sunny (too sunny), fast traffic

I want to live on abstract pain
Not like this. what the calendar has undressed
All my ghosts, bend down with strife
And everything a witness of the buried life

A date for the eleventh hour
Who needs that now. not I
The bright noon street the crooked faces
The flaming torch of December sinking sun

THE YET QUESTION

We ask the yet question,
Love naked tom-tom in America
When strong grain petal--
Wild & warm,
Diamond symphony women

God is a TV--
Eat magic moon ice & you
Can tell him no.

"from READ WHETHER (in-progress)"

to say, telephone or the coffee
or endless conversation. pure
serendipity, beautiful & divine,
like a Tulsa honeymoon or like
advice, like: "Descend with gravity
and doubt removed, the Moon
don't run on gasoline, the planets
creep like spaghetti on a lampshade"

Achtung! gamma rays, hydro pickles, a sort
of chromatic doorknob of the heart,
always present. roof. kerplunk. armstice.
pickle. pickle pickle pickle. it's
like it builds a hill at the base
of your brain, sometimes it rains.

BREAKFAST SONNET

The temple of your volcanic kiss is burning,
Edges charred, smoky air, submission
To an unfinished heart. Such comeliness
Flares cobalt blue, lemon, carmine red
Against my dull tones, fog and sand.
What night fenced in is poised between us,
Towering above the rest, above your
Curtained air, above my giltless charm,

River-daughter, real as you are real,
Hitting upon things--the chair, the cup--
Behind our studied loveliness, a flame-
Hurling devil angel, not unwelcome here--
Buried certain fathoms beneath the earth,
And above, down the abandoned heaven to us now.

ASCENSEUR POUR L'ECHAFAUD

but first one perfect twilight
in the middle of the river of
sunday april 15, 7:29 p.m.

(the Poet lives in the slums
of the reader's imaginary city)
it spreads out to the north & west

all green & gold, cold
in the fading light--there is no place
that the past can take place except
in right where you are looking at it now

I rebel against the tyranny of the calendar
The muses count onetwothreefourfive
Daughters of Time, count the sun
in the green limbs what do you see?

leaves like trembling jazz notes in a nightclub
you heard once, smoky nightclub air,
you were supposed to be somewhere else
that night what happened?

But you weren't. Life is what happens
while the girls circle the pier looking
for dropped bread crumbs for gleaming
silver fish scales the waves surge
up against the pilings wetting the legs
of the waders,
                          kush
                                kush.

LOVE, GONE AS LIGHTNING

so pick your terrain with that possibility in mind:
a million times over, to be born in the
silver light of the midnight moon, standing
among waterweeds, head cocked
benightedly

i would return to the sea with you
(possible even on the west coast)
on top of which, i eschew godly wisdom, thus:
"O my son, rise from thy bed / & work at what is wise"--
pfui! so maybe i don't wanna be wise!

CONFESSIONS OF ALEXANDER CALDER, 1898-1976
(confession #1)

beneath authentic pink honey Buddha
lighter than air, worshipped beneath
eternity, chanting like enlightened
demons eating the sky
& licking the animal sea

my dream is to be
present when near
some still enchanted happiness
Burning drolly, upon some more
unquiet spirit, attentive to
me alone
here

Jesus, red roses!
Would you think I'd want two?

BASEBALL IN THE DARK

The girl downstairs & the girl in Indiana
& the girl across town--green, past enchantment--
she isn't "in love"--Don & Matt playing baseball
on LSD in the dark (1993)--after a party--
last beer the whistle of the ball in the dark--

Little blue pills the color wheel the bare shoulder.
I have $8 & some change they turn off the gas tomorrow.
We are living in the Future it has a slightly metallic
sheen. I cannot date my checks it is all a little
wobbly, & cold too

All those old letters. Grain of salt! Points on a curve!
Flat beer & a book of wet matches I had the flu & couldn't
Church on Sunday, Bible & prayer book in red morocco
with
gilt edges. Cold supper in the evening And I almost felt
like crying myself just because he was crying

A drunken cheerleader peers through her fingers
Her boyfriend knows everything he has ever known
So do you

JACKET BLURB FOR *"HOW TO PICK UP WOMEN IN BARS AND OTHER OTHER PUBLIC PLACES"* BY DR. LOOMIS BURKHEAD, ED.D.

"Contains more than 1,500 weird, controversial, unconventional, arrogant, & outright strange opening strategies. From their tricky tactical surprises to their bizarre names, these openings fly in the face of tradition. You'll meet such openings as The Orangutan, The Raptor Variation, The Hallowe'en Gambit, Double Duck, The Frankenstein-Dracula Variations, & even The Drunken King. These openings are a sexy & exotic way to spice up a game & a great weapon to spring on unsuspecting & often unprepared opponents."

A WHITE BIRD

Gnarled briar pipe
On the shelf with
I-Ching coins,
Caller ID, nail
Clippers, green
Deco ashtray full
Of change, the
Bettie Page baseball
Card tilted to it,
A roach, mostly
Smoked, at her feet.

My girlfriend's hand
Passes over it, caught
In the lamp's halo,
A white bird dipping
Down so delicately down
Then upon the orange
Zig-Zags. And is gone.

CORRECTION

In the *Fall Arts Preview*
(September 12), a listing
for "Ted Berrigan's 'Sonnets,"
A November 15 tribute to the
Late poet, stated that
Berrigan (1934-1983)
Would be reading from
His own work.

The *Voice* regrets the error.

NOTE: The author of many of these poems was about half my age and had just fallen in love with writing poetry. The influences are pretty clear: Ted Berrigan, Ezra Pound, Alice Notley, Frank O'Hara, *Alice in Wonderl* and the *Wizard of Oz*, God, America, and, as now seems also clear, the Opposite Sex. Hence the title of the middle section, "Some Girls." Also the Stones. Author has decided to leave those as-is, rather than attempting somehow to update them. Apologies to all.

Made in the USA
Columbia, SC
16 September 2024

42435615R00065